# Fiddle Time Chris

T0055929

## a stockingful of 32 easy pieces for violin

Kathy and David Blackwell

illustrations by John Eastwood

Welcome to **Fiddle Time Christmas**. You'll find:

- 32 well-known Christmas carols and pieces with words to sing along
- solos and duets using finger patterns 0–1–23–4 and 0–12–3–4
- easy chord symbols for guitar or keyboard accompaniment; these chords are not compatible with the CD performances
- a CD with performances to listen or play along to; the varied accompaniments use piano, guitar, drums, and bass
- piano accompaniments available in a separate volume

Using the CD:

- all carols and pieces are played through twice, except those pieces which include a **D.C.** or **D.S. al Fine**, and 'Hogmanay Reel', which are performed once only
- each carol and piece has a short introduction and a link between the verses
- where there are duet parts, these are mostly added in the second verse
- Tuning track: track 33.

Performers: violin Olivier Bonnici; guitar Pete Vecchietti; double bass/bass guitar Mike Chilcott; percussion/drumkit Jon Buxton; piano David Blackwell. Grateful thanks to Pete Vecchietti for devising the CD arrangements of Nos. 2, 11, 25, and 30.

MUSIC DEPARTMENT

OXFORD
UNIVERSITY PRESS

OXFORD
UNIVERSITY PRESS

Great Clarendon Street, Oxford OX2 6DP, England

Oxford University Press is a department of the University of Oxford.
It furthers the University's aim of excellence in research, scholarship,
and education by publishing worldwide

Oxford is a registered trade mark of Oxford University Press
in the UK and in certain other countries

© Oxford University Press 2001 and 2010

Kathy and David Blackwell have asserted their rights under
the Copyright, Designs and Patents Act, 1988, to be identified as
Composers of this work

Database right Oxford University Press (maker)

First published 2001. Revised edition published 2010
Photocopying or arranging this copyright material is ILLEGAL

All rights reserved. No part of this publication may be reproduced,
stored in a retrieval system, or transmitted, in any form or by any means,
without the prior permission in writing of Oxford University Press,
or as expressly permitted by law. Enquiries concerning reproduction
outside the scope of the above should be sent to the Music Copyright
Department, Oxford University Press, at the address above

Permission to perform these works in public
(except in the course of divine worship) should normally be obtained
from the Performing Right Society Ltd (PRS), 29/33 Berners Street,
London W1T 3AB, or its affiliated Societies in each country throughout
the world, unless the owner or the occupier of the premises
being used holds a licence from the Society

Permission to make a recording must be obtained in advance
from the Mechanical-Copyright Protection Society Ltd (MCPS),
Elgar House, 41 Streatham High Road, London SW16 1ER,
or its affiliated Societies in each country throughout the world

10

ISBN 978-0-19-336933-7

Music and text origination by
Barnes Music Engraving Ltd, East Sussex
Printed in Great Britain on acid-free paper by
Halstan & Co. Ltd, Amersham, Bucks.

# Contents


| Piece/ track no. | | Page no. |
|---|---|---|
| 1 | Hark! the herald-angels sing | 4 |
| 2 | Mary had a baby | 4 |
| 3 | The holly and the ivy (*duet*) | 5 |
| 4 | Ding dong! merrily on high | 6 |
| 5 | Andrew mine, Jasper mine | 6 |
| 6 | Silent night (*duet*) | 7 |
| 7 | I saw three ships (*duet*) | 8 |
| 8 | O little town of Bethlehem | 8 |
| 9 | Christmas Calypso (*duet*) | 9 |
| 10 | Once in royal David's city | 10 |
| 11 | Go tell it on the mountain | 10 |
| 12 | O Christmas tree (*duet*) | 11 |
| 13 | We wish you a merry Christmas | 12 |
| 14 | Shepherds watched | 12 |
| 15 | We three kings | 13 |
| 16 | O come, all ye faithful (*duet*) | 14 |
| 17 | Bethl'em lay a-sleeping (*duet*) | 15 |
| 18 | Good King Wenceslas | 15 |
| 19 | Deck the hall | 16 |
| 20 | Away in a manger (*duet*) | 17 |
| 21 | The first Nowell | 17 |
| 22 | Zither Carol | 18 |
| 23 | God rest you merry, gentlemen | 18 |
| 24 | While shepherds watched their flocks | 19 |
| 25 | Children, go! (*duet*) | 19 |
| 26 | Skaters' Waltz (*duet*) | 20 |
| 27 | Dance of the Reed Pipes | 21 |
| 28 | Jingle, bells | 22 |
| 29 | Infant holy, infant lowly (*duet*) | 22 |
| 30 | Child in a manger (*duet*) | 23 |
| 31 | Hogmanay Reel | 24 |
| 32 | Auld Lang Syne | 24 |
| 33 | Tuning track (A—D—G—E) | |

## 1. Hark! the herald-angels sing

Felix Mendelssohn (1809–47)

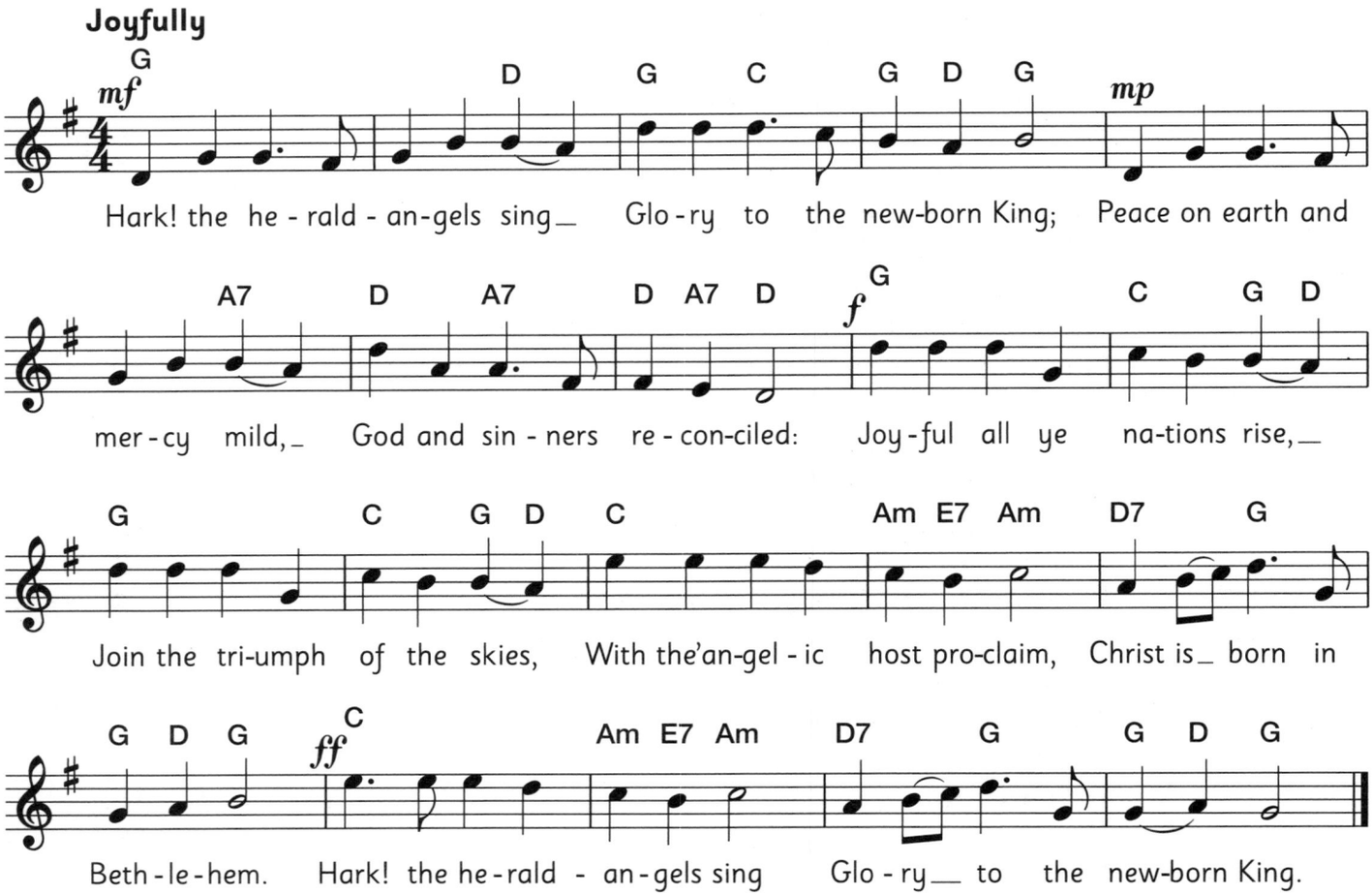


## 2. Mary had a baby

American trad.

# 3. The holly and the ivy

English trad.

# 4. Ding dong! merrily on high

16th-century French melody

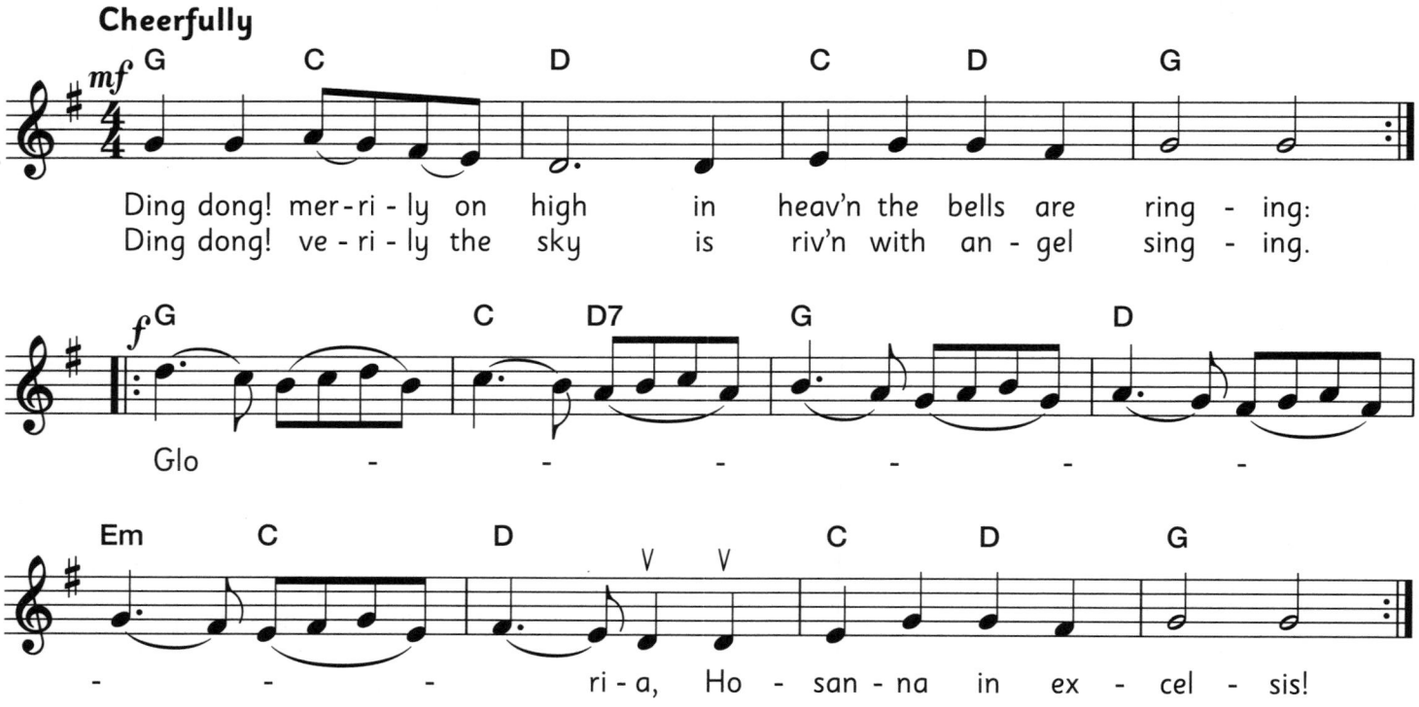


# 5. Andrew mine, Jasper mine

Moravian carol

*Andrew mine, Jasper mine*: words by C. K. Offer from *Three Moravian Carols*

© Oxford University Press 1962. Reproduced by permission of Oxford University Press.

# 6. Silent night

Franz Gruber (1787–1863)

# 7. I saw three ships

English trad.

**Like a dance**

*f* G D

I saw three ships come sail - ing in On Christ-mas Day, on Christ-mas Day, I

*mf*

G D G

saw three ships come sail - ing in On Christ-mas Day in the morn - ing.

# 8. O little town of Bethlehem

English trad.

**Gently**

*mp* A7 D A D A D G A7 D

O lit - tle town of Beth - le - hem, How still we_ see thee lie!
A - bove thy deep and dream-less sleep The si - lent stars go by.

*mf* F#m A7 D A D G A A7

Yet_ in thy dark streets shin - eth The ev - er - last - ing light; The

*mp* D A D A D G A7 D

hopes and fears of all__ the_ years Are met in__ thee to - night.

# 9. Christmas Calypso

Kathy & David Blackwell

**Happily**

*f*

So dance the Christ-mas Ca-lyp-so in the sun,

*f*

Je-sus is born for ev-'ry-one; Sing out with joy and

stamp your feet, move to the ca-lyp-so beat!

**Fine**

*mf*

Way back in Beth-le-hem, in a sim-ple sta-ble,

*mf*

Je-sus, that ba-by boy, came to save us all! So dance the

**D.𝄋 al Fine**

## 10. Once in royal David's city

H. J. Gauntlett (1805–76)

## 11. Go tell it on the mountain

American trad.

# 12. O Christmas tree

German trad.

# 13. We wish you a merry Christmas trad. West Country

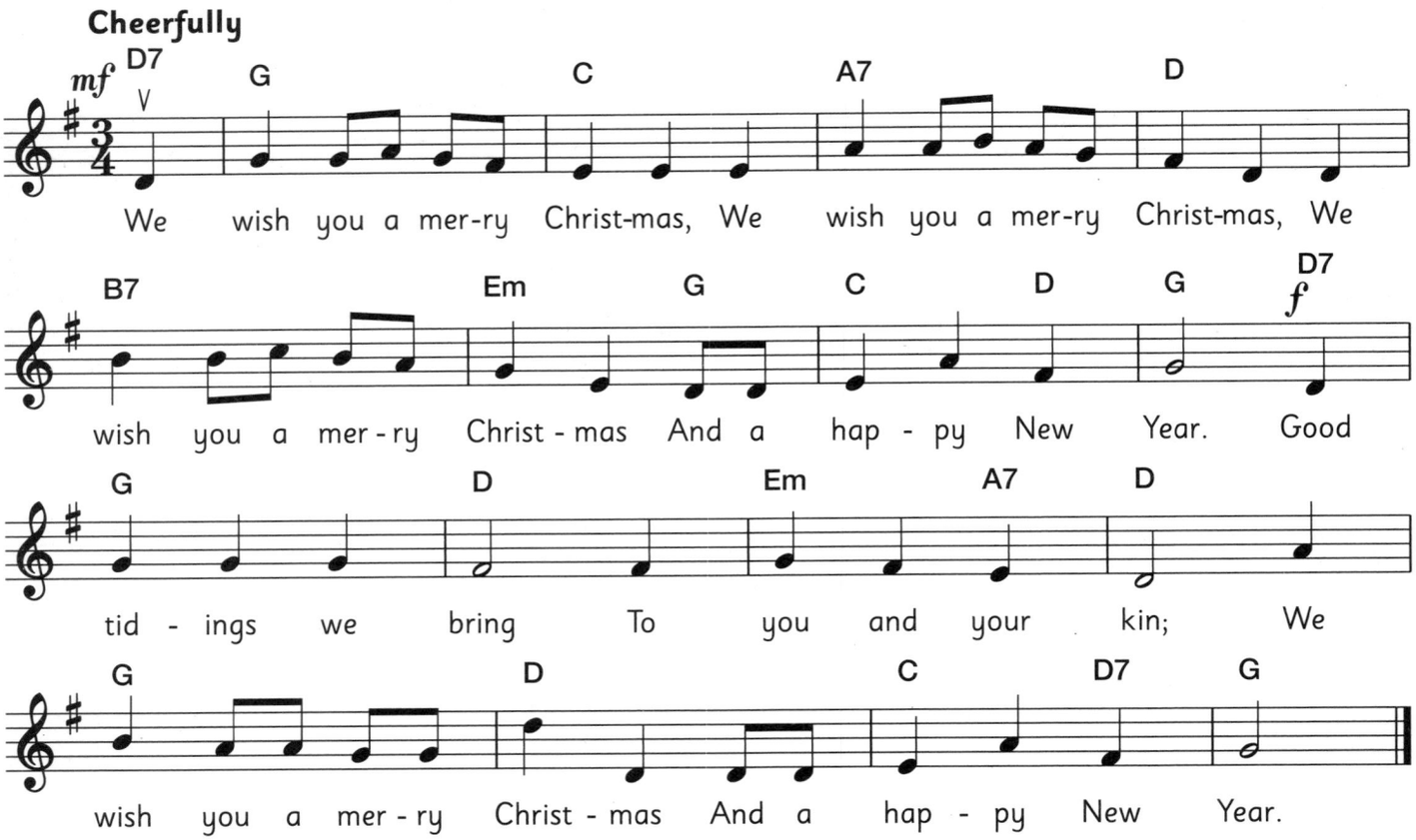


# 14. Shepherds watched Czech carol

# 15. We three kings

J. H. Hopkins (1820–91)

**Stately**

Em B7 Em

*mp*

We three kings of O - ri - ent are; Bear - ing gifts we

B7 Em *mf* D G

tra - verse a - far Field and foun - tain, moor and moun - tain,

Am B7 Em D7 G

*f*

Fol - low - ing yon - der star: O_____ star of won - der,

C G C G Em

star of night, Star with roy - al beau - ty bright, West - ward

D C D G C G

lead - ing, still pro - ceed - ing, Guide us to thy per - fect light.

# 16. O come, all ye faithful

J. F. Wade (*c.*1711–86)

**Joyfully**

*mf* G D G C G D Em D A

O come, all ye faith - ful, Joy - ful and tri - um - phant, O come ye, O

*mf*

D G D A7 D *f* G C D7 G

come_ ye to Beth - le - hem; Come and be - hold him

*f*

D Em Am D (no chord) *mp* *mf*

Born the King of An - gels: O come, let us a - dore him, O come, let us a -

*mf*

*f* G C D Em Am G D7 G

- dore him, O come let us a - dore him,_ Christ___ the Lord!

*f*

# 17. Bethl'em lay a-sleeping

Polish carol

# 18. Good King Wenceslas

*Piae Cantiones* (1582)

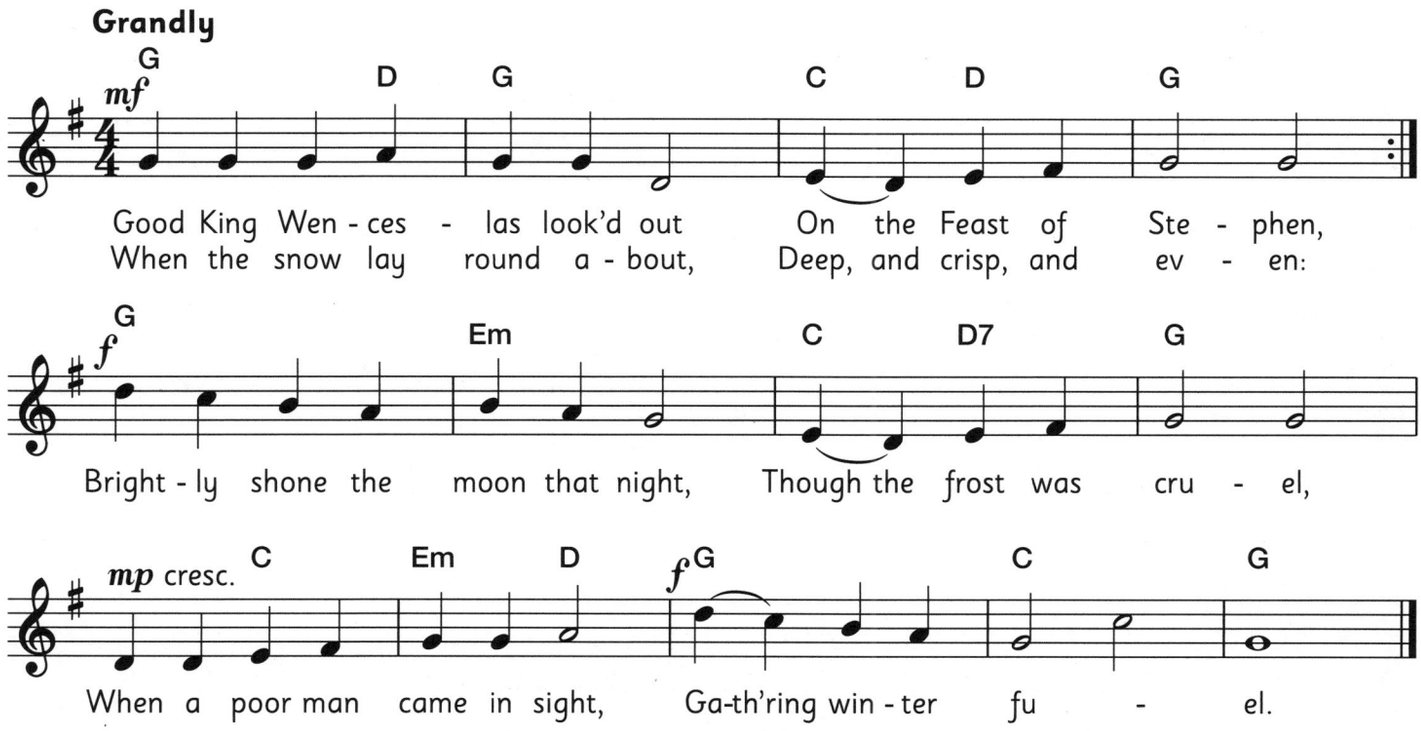

## 19. Deck the hall

Welsh trad.

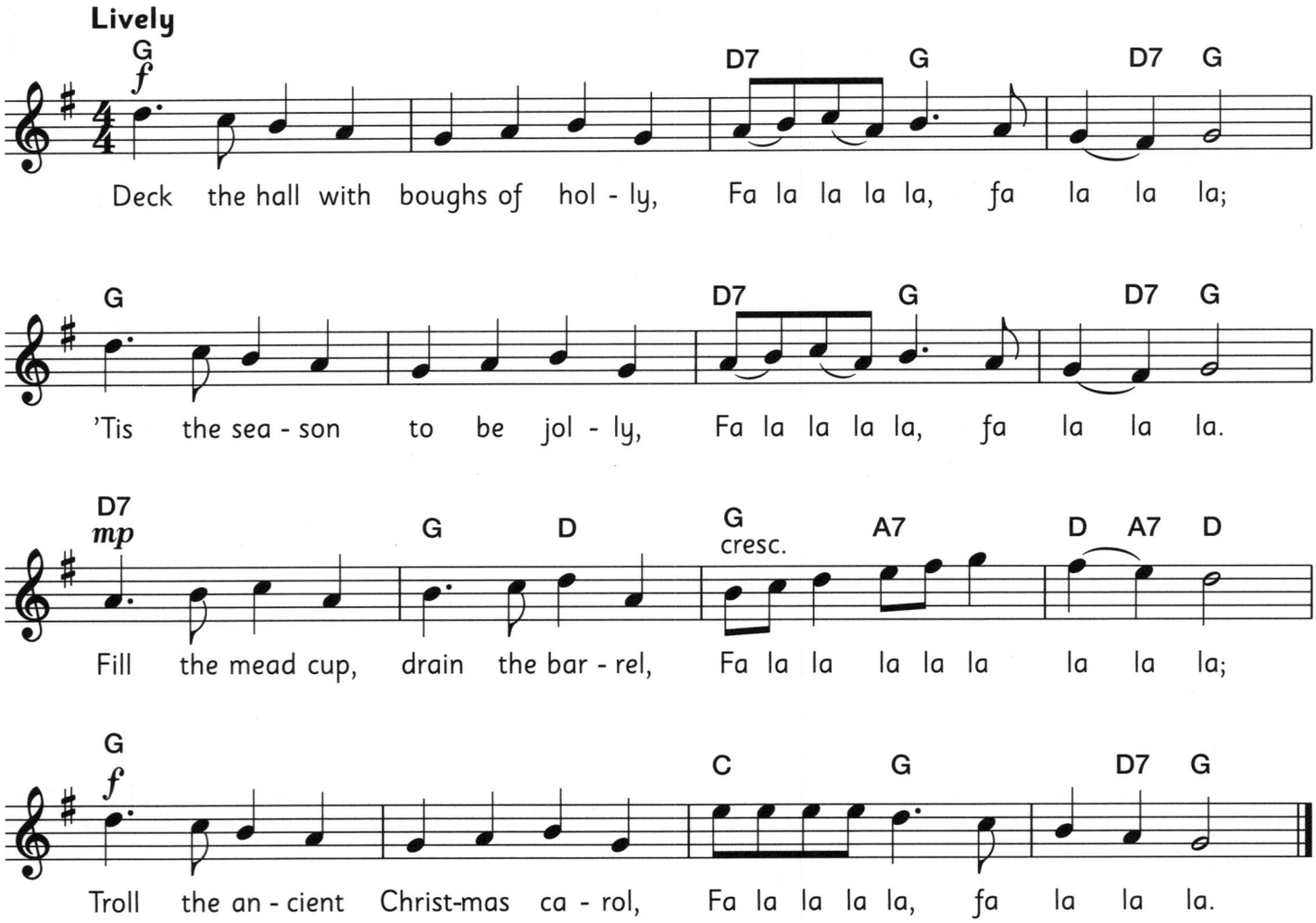

## 20. Away in a manger

William J. Kirkpatrick (1838–1921)

## 21. The first Nowell

English trad.

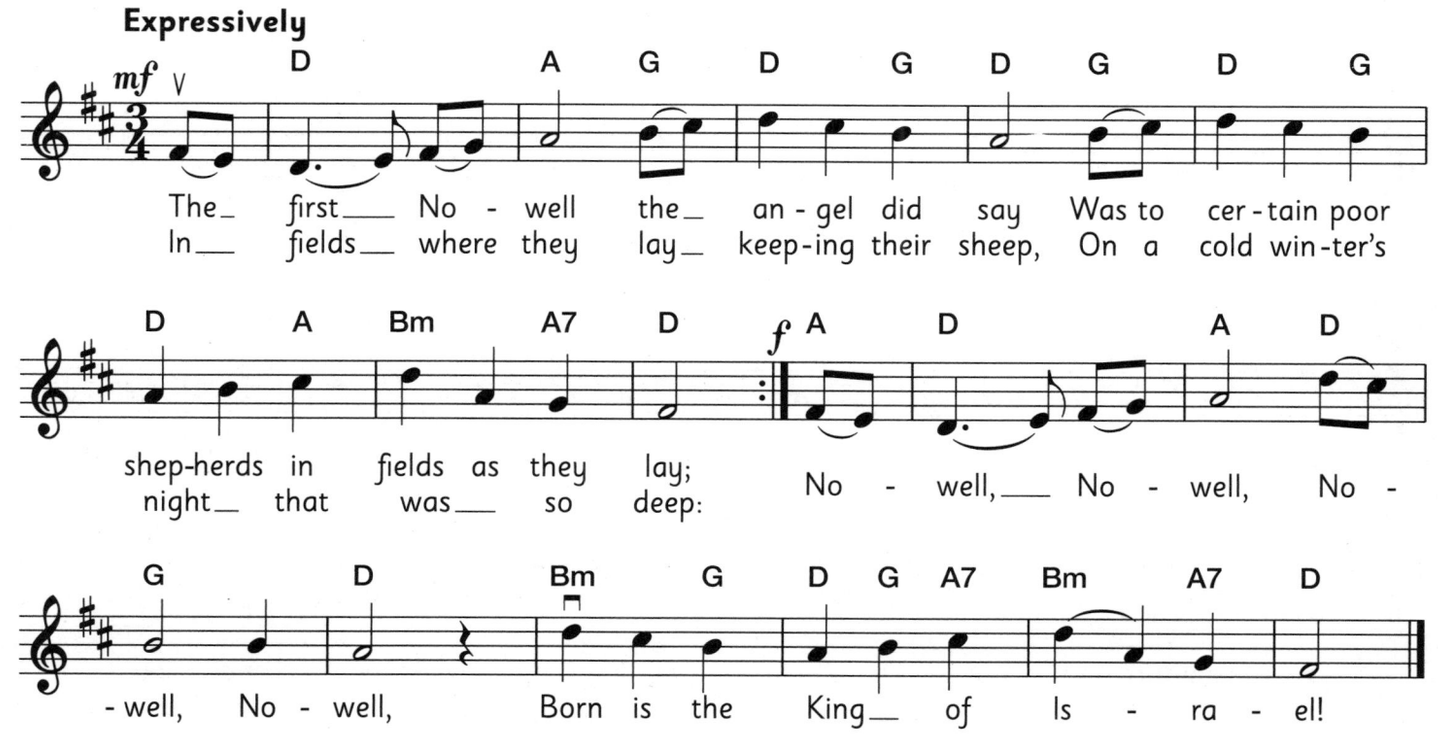

# 22. Zither Carol

Czech carol

# 23. God rest you merry, gentlemen

English trad.

# 24. While shepherds watched their flocks

*Este's Psalter* (1592)

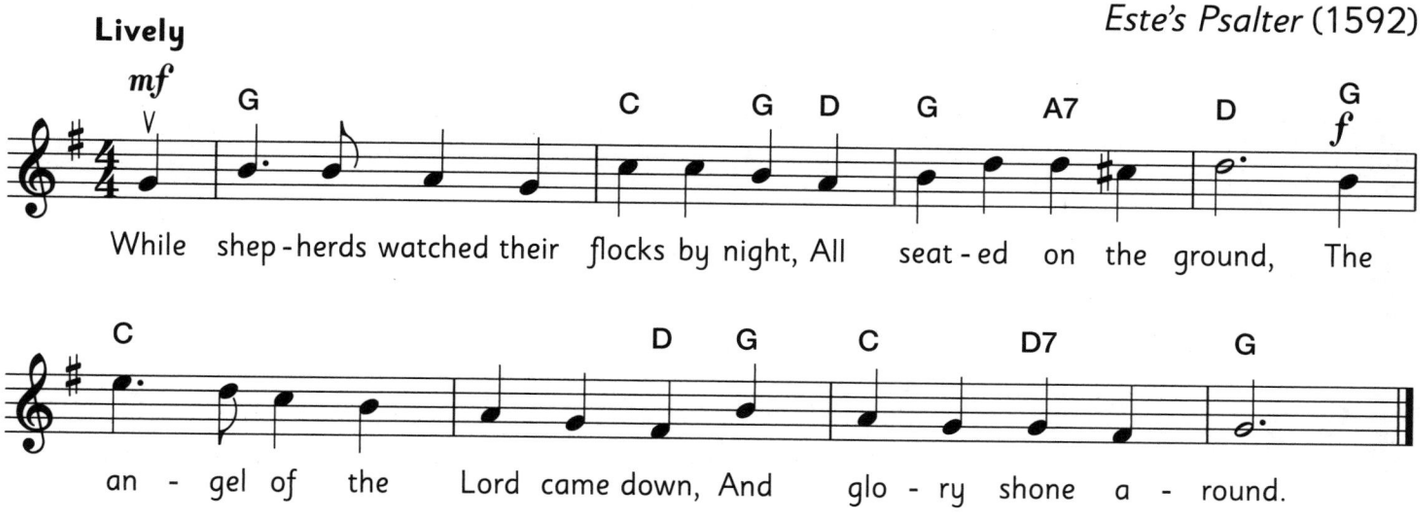

# 25. Children, go!

Spiritual

# 26. *Skaters' Waltz*

Emil Waldteufel (1837–1915)

# 27. Dance of the Reed Pipes

(from the *Nutcracker* ballet)

Pyotr Ilyich Tchaikovsky (1840–93)

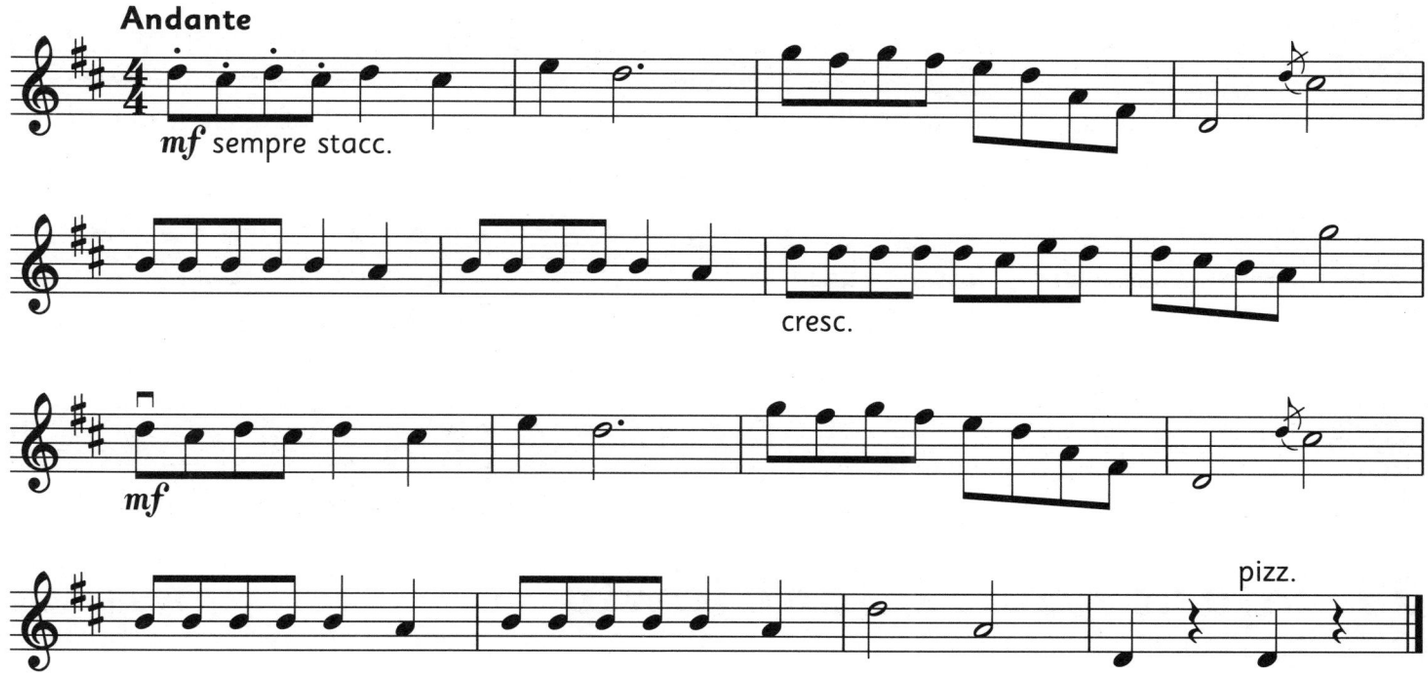

# 28. Jingle, bells

J. Pierpont (1822–93)

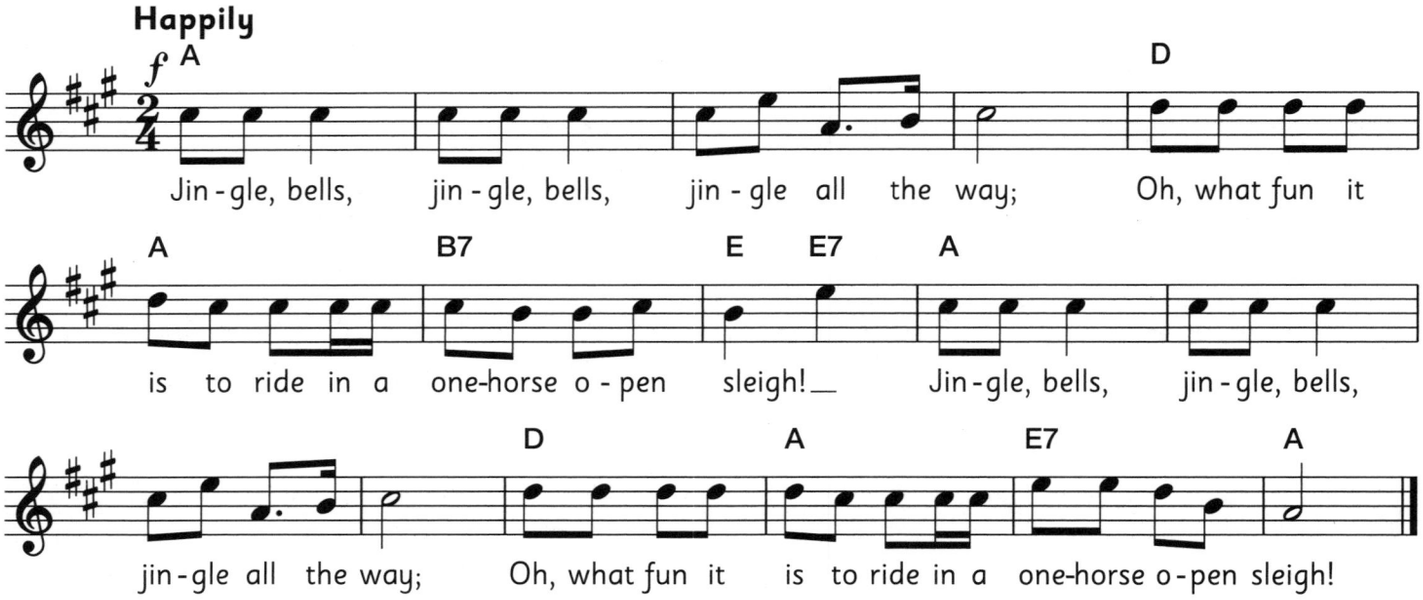


# 29. Infant holy, infant lowly

Polish carol

# 30. Child in a manger

Celtic trad.

# 31. Hogmanay Reel

Kathy & David Blackwell

**With energy**

# 32. Auld Lang Syne

Scottish trad.

**With a wee dram!**